# Rhymes & Ballads from Berry Bay

by

Randall Hans Crone

June 23/97.

To Jim & Marvin
fr Doug & Max

Illustrations
by
Robert Southern

# Rhymes & Ballads from Berry Bay

Randall Hans Crone

BOREAL PUBLISHING

**Canadian Cataloguing in Publication Data**

Crone, Randall Hans, 1952 -
Rhymes & ballads From Berry Bay

Poems.
ISBN 0-9680538-2-3

I. Title. II. Title: Rhymes & ballads from Berry Bay.

PS8555.R61115R59 1997 C811'.54 C97-900407-1
PR9199.3.C688R59 1997

Illustrations: Robert M. Southern

Printed and bound in Canada by Hignell Printing

## ACKNOWLEDGEMENTS

This work could not have been accomplished without the inspiration and encouragement provided by Ms. Lori Ann Power.

Many thanks to Ms. Esther Power for relating life experiences of a pioneer in Herb Town.

Thanks to Zoe Irvine and Chris Wakeling of Boreal Publishing for the guidance, advice and professional objectivity.

Much appreciation is extended to Louise and Bob Cooper; Lillian and Jim Haines; and Marc, Leone, Joel and Jessica Jackson for human contact and hearty food.

I would also like to thank and congratulate the special community of *Snow Lake on their 50th Anniversary* of pioneering perseverance.

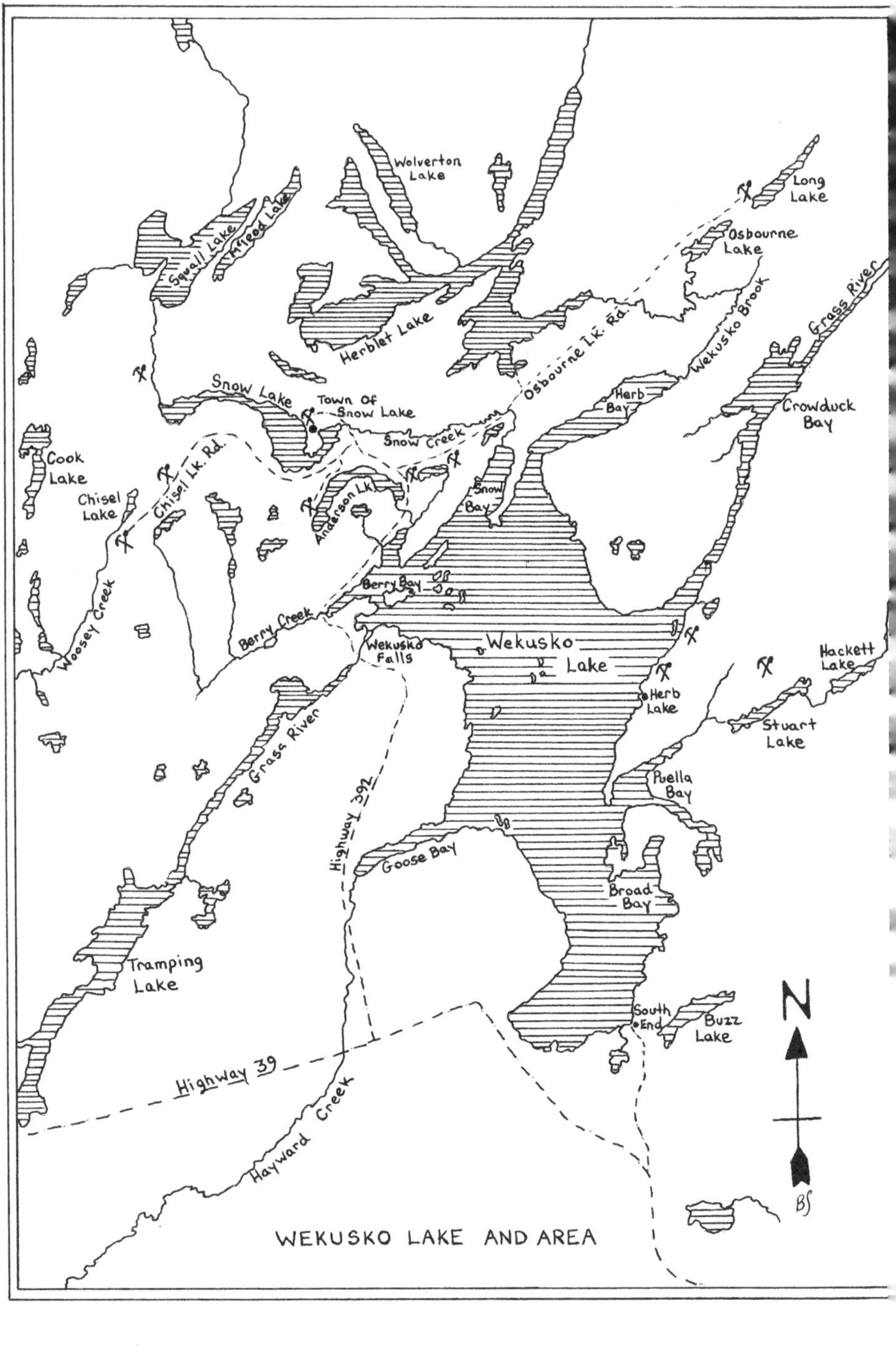


WEKUSKO LAKE AND AREA

## DEDICATION

This book is dedicated to the hardy pioneers of days long past and the special breed of Northerners who presently survive and prosper in this untamed land of beauty.

CONTENTS

## THREE DREAMERS

The nine-fingered miner, with a dirty one liner,
Laughed as he strolled to the cage.
He spat as he spoke, gave his partner a poke,
His eyes were wild and ablaze.
"I'd give my good arm for ten acres of farm,
A place for some cattle to graze,
A range I can roam, a place to call home,
A good woman who means what she says."

With a nod of his head, the cage tender said,
"I couldn't agree with you more.
A kettle of fish and a dory's my wish,
Brought in from the briny north shore.
And if I were a man with riches in hand,
I'd buy that damn boat, hellbent!
But with wages these days and the bonus they pay,
I'm lucky to make next month's rent."

With a shrug of chagrin, wiping grease off his chin,
The blaster gave way to a thought.
"But if we were rich men, would we be then,
Owners of the dreams we have sought?
Would we find peace, joy and release
From the worries and woes of our time,
Or would we remain, essentially the same,
Content in the depths of this mine?"

So together we went in dark, deep descent,
The fisherman, farmer and I,
Searching for gold and the commerce bestowed,
As the levels quickly rolled by.
We laughed as we spoke of blasting and smoke,
Normal events of our day.
Of acres of grass and oceans so vast,
And the quest for another week's pay.

## THIS LAND

I love this land
its piney stand, where craggy rock meets shore,
fir and spruce, caribou and moose,
where eagle and osprey soar.

I love this land
its untamed brand, its legends and its lore,
where shaggy bear and snow white hare
hear ancient rapids roar.

I love this land
its wild command, loons calling out in jest,
grey wolves howl, a great horned owl
screeches from lofty nest.

I love this land
its starry band of Northern Lights on high,
the dancing rays of frosty haze
envelop earth and sky.

## SLIM ROACH

Slim Roach lived south of Herb Town, along a hillside stream
That trickled gentle waters to the garden of his dreams.
The sight of it amazed him, and he gave his head a scratch,
A ten-acre back-breaker veg-e-table patch.

Slim Roach loved his garden, and his garden loved to grow
To incredible proportions; Slim Roach had proudly sown
Five acres of potatoes, four tomatoes and three beets,
With turnips and parsnips as long as sasquatch feet!

Slim Roach set to digging in the far side of the hill,
A cellar for the veggies from the earth he loved to till.
For length he made it twice as long as any giant's stride,
Deeper than a spruce tree's roots and nearly thrice as wide.

Slim Roach dug out his cellar till the sweat rolled off his back,
Dreaming of a harvest that would fill the largest sack.
When earthen floor was trampled and the job was deemed complete,
He stuffed his chops to bursting with a raw and juicy beet.

Slim Roach loved his garden, and he tended it with care,
And for his veggie shelter, Slim built a tiny stair.
With smile that creased his leathery face, he worked the daylight hours,
Bursting with raw vigour from a surge of veggie power!

Slim Roach then laid his bedroll on the ground that he loved best,
Watched the Northern Lights above his fertile garden nest,
Guarded it with tenderness till harvest time was done,
A veggie vigilante with an old squirrel gun.

Slim Roach lived a singular, a solitary life,
Too eccentric, I suppose, to win himself a wife.
He never built a home to house his lonely bachelor's bed,
Slept happily and comfortably with vegetables instead.

*Slim Roach was one Herb Lake Pioneer who grew a good garden. He had a root cellar to keep his potatoes in but couldn't see the necessity for a house. So, he just spread his bedroll on top of the potatoes, and there he slept.*

*Excerpt from the chap book: <u>Snow Lake's Centennial Salute to the Trailblazers</u>*

## FEED ME

Caring and sharing through life's twists and turns,
Love pounds through my veins and in my brain burns
The sight and the scent of your body so fine,
Give me your all, and on it I'll dine,
And never go hungry, I'll never be cold,
So lay down beside me and let me be bold,
Have me and hold me, ravage my soul,
Your eyes green as jade, your hair black as coal.

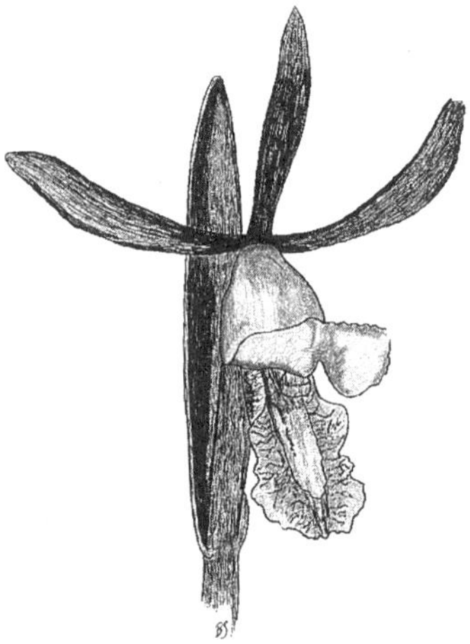

## KATE AND DICK

At spring's early thaw, she mushed to Le Pas,
In the year of nineteen-o-nine,
Taught school for a year and then disappeared
Right into the heart of the pines.
She paddled canoe down river and slough,
A woman alone in the world.
With moxy that showed, she searched for the gold,
Heart pounding and spirit unfurled.

Through Cranberry Lakes, she steadily took
The Grass River route to the east,
With rifle at side, took aim and with pride,
Had squirrel and ptarmigan feast.
As winter set in, her grubstake ran thin,
She raided more traps than a few.
In December she froze both fingers and toes;
The North is not kind to the new.

A strong, hardy breed, she still felt the need
Of a partner to help stake her claim.
She stumbled upon a trail that went on
For miles over country untamed.
She struggled forth in this land of the north,
Set traps and hunted for game,
Till covered in frost and hopelessly lost,
She heard someone call out her name.

"Miss Rice, to the left, where the rocks form a cleft,
There's a path to my cabin of logs.
My name is Dick Woosey, and if you're not choosy,
You can sleep by my fire with the dogs.
I'm quite a good cook, I've read a few books,
And I know the lay of this land.
Stay with me here in this chilly frontier;
Together we'll make a strong stand."

With frostbitten cheek and a mood far from meek,
Kate spoke as she sat by the fire,
"I know you to hold a mad passion for gold,
But I've never heard tell you're a liar;
So I'll eat up your grub, and I'll tell you this, Bub,
It's nickel and zinc I desire.
It's partners we'll be, both equal and free
To prospect this land of the lakes,
Through Burntwood and Hayes, the ore fairly lays,
Waiting for us to claim stake."

They staked out their claims, together their names
Imbedded on rugged pine posts.
When time comes to pay respect for their day,
We salute them with pioneer toasts.
For Woosey and Rice have paid the full price
Of the prospector's lust for the lode,
A hardy, true breed, they nurtured the creed,
And honoured the Northerner's Code.

## MINER MEN

Clank of wrench, diesel stench, hard hat and a lamp,
Darkened stope, drillers cope, jackleg cold and damp,
Shoulders wet, slick with sweat, do work few others can,
Hard workin', hard rockin', greasy miner men.

Clang of steel, slashes peeled, follow shifter's maps,
Load the ring, Amex sting, B-Line to the caps,
Guard the pass, fiery blast, muck the ore to bins,
Hard workin', hard rockin', greasy miner men.

Weary hours, hit the showers, day is done at last,
Hoist a few, frosty brew, music of the past,
Hug the kids, hit the skids, find comfort at day's end,
Hard workin', hard rockin', greasy miner men.

## HIDDEN HAZARDS

The driller and helper went down to the site
Where the Dimac lay waiting to drill through the night.
Steel rods were standing, row upon row,
The core tubes were cleaned and ready to go.
So they pumped down the water and started to drill,
The thirty foot core barrel started to fill.
    The whine of the ram and the hum of the bore;
    Music to the ears of those who cut core.

There wasn't a warning, it happened so fast,
A bright flash of fire and a thunderous blast
Ripped the machine right off of the sloop,
Threw it like driftwood into the scoop,
Smashing the helper into the wheel,
Pinning the driller under cold steel.
    The cut-out soon filled with the dust and the smoke,
    The driller lay helpless and started to choke.

The helper was blind with the flash of the blast,
His ribs were all broken, his strength ebbing fast.
He made for the valve and cranked on the air,
He knew that the smoke would kill them right there.
He crawled to his partner, in shock with the pain,
Tried lifting the drill, an effort in vain.
    So he lay down beside this miner of gold
    And talked to him softly till his body grew cold.

The rescue team rallied and ran to the site
Where searchers of gold had worked their last night.
They tested for gas, then lifted the drill,
Laid bodies on stretchers, lifeless and still.
With hearts grave and heavy, feet made of lead,
The rescuers marched with their cargo of dead
    Into the station and onto the cage,
    Weighing the price of a working man's wage.

## CROSSES WE BEAR

All of us have crosses to bear,
losses to share,
we've all heard anguished cries
from friends in black mourning;
death's hidden warning
that none of the pain
lay buried there.

We've all felt the seed
of malice and greed,
and we all have sinister sins
that pass in repentance;
lurk in remembrance,
insidious omen you
better well heed.

We've all had the urge,
the hunger and surge,
we've all felt invisible bonds
of love at its peak;
sweet emotion we seek
and cannot deny, nor have
the power to purge.

We've yearned for our share
of days that were fair,
all of us have searched for the truth
to set our souls free;
so at long last they'd be
at peace with
our lords of despair.

## GENTLE BREEZE

gentle breeze lifts feathered wings
upon its unseen might,
swaying spruce through forest glen,
carries on its willful wend,
to bend the reeds and spill their seeds
aloft in pillowed flight.

## THE LEGEND OF BIG JACK LARUE

All sickly and thin, the madman burst in
On the cabin of Big Jack Larue.
For Jack, it was known, had seeded and grown,
The herbs to cure sickness and flu.

With hungover eyes, the madman he cries,
"Find me a permanent cure
For all of my woes, or I'm destined to go
Stark raving mad to be sure.

The years of abuse, the beers and misuse
Of toxins not meant for mankind,
Have taken their toll on body and soul,
And left me quite out of my mind."

Big Jack perceived all, and he answered the call,
Started peeling the mould off green sticks.
With a look unperturbed, he threw in a few herbs,
Stirred turpentine into the mix.

When it came to a boil, Jack added some oil
That fumed with a horrible stench.
He minced up the meat from old beavers' feet,
And stirred it all up with a wrench.

Through white-crackled lips, the madman took sips
Of the broth the trapper had boiled.
With nothing to lose, only one course to choose,
He choked back the brew and recoiled.

He paused at the brink, then got past the stink,
Tossed it all down in a gulp.
At the taste of the blend, his hair stood on end;
He spat out great pieces of pulp.

He started to swear as he danced in the air,
His skin turned all clammy and hot.
He tore at his ears, his eyes filled with tears,
His nose ran runny with snot.

He coughed and he gagged, sputtered and sagged
To his knees at the foot of the bed.
Shrieked at Larue as he spewed out foul brew,
"I fear that you've killed me instead."

His head jerked once more as he slid to the floor,
And his eyes rolled back in his head.
He grunted and groaned, farted and moaned,
Then lay there as if he were dead.

The trapper looked down, brow furrowed with frown,
Then placed the poor man on a cot.
Mused with concern: There's much to be learned
'Bout healing, like it or not.

So Big Jack Larue concocted a stew
Of ptarmigan, muskrat and grouse.
He added some plants, some herbs and red ants,
Then he threw in a little grey mouse.

A caribou's nose, three feet and some toes
Of a frog went into the brew,
A wolf's mouldy ear and a raven's black rear,
Completed Jack's bilious stew.

"I must be quite sure that I finish the cure,"
Said Jack to himself as he cooked.
"This man is real sick and I gotta be quick,
Or he'll be as dead as he looks."

With Samaritan care, Jack tended him there,
And taught him the way of the land.
In time he got well, that madman from hell,
Thanks be to Jack's healing hand.

## PIONEER BILLY TODD

The summer he canoed to Wekusko's west shore,
Pioneer Billy was a young man no more.
He followed the trail traced by Samuel Hearne,
True northern blood in Billy's heart burned.

He paddled his canoe up the Grass River route,
Witnessed bull moose eat green willow shoot.
He prospered and thrived at nature's command;
Pioneer Bill loved this wild northern land.

He walked virgin forests devoid of human trace,
He drank from crystal waters at rapids' foamy base.
Mastering nature while searching for gold,
Billy Todd had to be both brazen and bold.

A two-bit trapper's cabin was his humble abode
While Billy Todd searched for the great mother lode,
His passion for this country knew no human bounds,
Traversing Grassy River, Billy Todd drowned.

Spirits mark his passing with candle-lit wake,
Northern Lights shimmer over Ospwagan Lake,
Poplar and birch guard his watery grave,
Billy Todd's creed: Live free; be brave.

## SEASONS

Brown withered leaves 'gainst grey clouded sky
Rudely remind me that summer's gone by.
The crystalline frost that forms in the night
Struggles to stay through day's early light.
A cold northern wind whips at your clothes,
Warning of winter and forthcoming snows.

The sun starts to weaken, losing its powers,
As the ground grows colder, my attitude sours
Towards changing seasons, bright days turn dull,
Grey jays and chickadees replacing the gull
Who's flown with the mallards and geese going south.
Feel the chill in my bones, taste the frost on my mouth.

## HOG LOVERS

"Tank" was even bigger that his nickname would suppose,
Muscles bulged his beefy arms like thickened rubber hose.
He grabbed hold of his Harley, then kicked the bike to life,
Hugged both his smiling children, very slowly kissed his wife,
Then settled in the saddle, amid cold steel and chrome,
Waved a biker's slow salute and rumbled from his home.

Harvey rode a shovelhead, two barrels of the best,
Nitrous oxide powerhouse, beat all who faced the test.
He idled down his iron horse and looked back on his farm,
Gazed upon the girl he'd wed, his baby in her arms,
With final kiss and squeal of tire, the biker jams the gears,
The thunder of the V-twin stroke sweet music to his ears.

Big Tank, he was a city man; a farm was Harvey's home,
Free spirits with a common cause, a foreign road to roam.
We rounded up at halfway house on highway 39,
Nitrous Harv, big Tank and I, three destinies entwined.
Bikers cruise the open road, take trouble in their stride,
Leather-clad barbarians; I call them friends with pride.

## DON' WANNA DIE

Don' wanna die by smoke or by fire,
Don' wanna die at the hands of a liar,
Don' wanna death that's noble or grand,
I don' wanna die by my own hand,
Don' wanna die from gunshot or knife,
Don' wanna take credit for another man's life.
'Cause sometimes I feel like earth freshly tilled,
Disturbed and dark, I wait to be filled
With sunshine and rain and crops to be milled.
Don' wanna die
Till the good Lord wills.

## DEAR BROTHER (C.W.C. 1964-1996)

A young mind in torment
Is a most fragile thing,
From light to dark
Its momentum will swing,
Until a time when there is no light,
No strength to survive, nor to hope, nor to fight;
All crushed by the gloom and the doom of your plight.

Oh brother, dear brother,
At last you've found peace,
All your pain and your torment
Have found their release,
And as those left behind in the wake of your death
Gather round your cold body, I utter this breath
Of anguish and grief, despair and denial;
How could something so precious be treated so vile?

Young brother, dead brother,
I grieve for you, son,
Now tally the score
And reveal what was won
In this battle of life, what honour bestowed,
Who was the victor; the victim we know,
Who reaps rewards for these seeds that we sow;
In ice-cold compassion, I feel the tears flow.

## WILD ORCHID

Elegant beauty of soft, subtle shade,
Four perfect petals in lush ferny glade,
Crowned with the golden sunshine that plays
Amongst the gardens nature has made.

Glistening diamonds, mid-morning dew,
Reflecting your aura of rainbow's hue,
Giving you life, so fragile you grew
Into an orchid, so free; so few.

Precious wild orchid on green leafy vine,
Drink of this life, love's bitter-sweet wine,
Spread forth your petals, embrace the divine,
Bask in the glory while summer still shines.

And fear not the winter's cold, killing snow,
Fear not the north winds, although they will blow,
Fear not the raven's bold, raucous crow,
Fear not the things that you do not know.

For I will not pluck you to cast you aside,
And I will not crush you under my stride,
I will not question the tears that you've cried,
I'll not say I love you, then tell you I lied.

## BIG DAN

Big Dan the driller man had half his thumb gone,
Pinched off in the jaws when the air was turned on.
He screamed and he cussed and he spat and he bled,
Big Dan the driller man turned ten shades of red.

"Partner, it seems that you've wounded me some,"
Said Dan to this man who was holding his thumb.
"I told you quite clearly to turn OFF the air,
Now look at my thumb!" he yelled with a glare.

He wrapped it in burlap, teeth set in a clench,
Big Dan the driller man grabbed hold of a wrench.
"You said most distinctly to turn ON the air,"
I pleaded, retreating from Dan and his stare.

He said, "Whoa, little partner, it's only a scratch,
A piece of this hose and a clamp make a patch.
We'll tighten it down and get back to work,
Can't let the boys think we're starting to shirk."

So he set back to work with his thumb in a clamp,
The hose and the burlap all bloody and damp.
He finished his round 'fore the end of the shift,
Big Dan the driller man walked down the drift.

He was stubborn and rude, he'd brag in the showers
'Bout the bonus he earned, the long, weary hours.
He never talked politics, union or art,
His body was built 'round a contractor's heart.

Others agreed he had license to boast,
Worked hard as he could; that's harder than most.
Bloody and greasy and stinking of sweat,
Big Dan the driller man's match can't be met.

## THE CAGE

Their head lamps for shiners, the hard rockin' miners
Hammer the ore vein with steel.
With scoop tram for muckin', they rarely stop truckin',
Mining holds special appeal.

This pioneer breed from strong, hardy seed,
Experts in their special craft,
Drill the next round and then, homeward bound,
Trudge to the mouth of the shaft.

All beaten and battered, the cage with a clatter
Descends to the earth's very core.
To the miners' delight, it glides into sight,
And the cage tender opens the door.

"Three bells and all's well, let's ride up from hell,
You greasy old miners of ore.
You've slaved for your wage, get in the damn cage,
And we'll rise to the surface once more."

Their hard hats all muddy, slickers all cruddy,
The sweat of them smelling like socks,
The miners all stand with lunch pails in hand,
Sardines in a little tin box.

The hoistman on surface, his duty and purpose,
To answer the cage tender's bell,
When mining men ride with patience and pride;
Another day finished in hell.

## COLD WATERS

The harsh, cold waters of Hudson Bay
Stole the life of a boy today.
Tricked by tides that do not care,
A child could find no mercy there.

His parents mourned in black refrain,
Their joy in life left to remain
Under the waters off Churchill's coast,
A lonely grave for a young boy's ghost.

Would it be fate or is it God's way
To end the life of a boy through play?
In deathly games, nobody wins;
An icy tomb, no prayers, no hymns.

## ODE TO MISS RICE

I never knew Miss Kathleen Rice, but legends tell the tale
Of fortunes that were promised and dreams that could not fail,
Of life upon an island that bears her worthy name,
A solitary pioneer, she clearly staked her claim.

The island that she proudly named stands stark against the sky,
She made her camp on mossy earth and felt her spirit fly,
For freedom and the search for gold had mixed within her veins,
She stripped the soil from Mother Earth to coax out yellow grains.

The spirit of this northern land grew strong within her breast,
As she steered her fragile craft through rapids' raging crest,
Her paddle plunged down deep and strong to berth the stony crags,
Faced the wrath of Sturgeon Weir; her courage never sagged.

Landing canoe at water's edge she quelled her beating heart,
Pushing on with iron will she beat cruel winter's start,
She followed Grassy River route to make Wekusko's shore,
With pioneering fortitude that filled her very core.

I never knew Miss Kathleen Rice, but legends tell the tale,
While Northern Lights illuminate her pioneering trail,
Of courage and of bravery in volumes do they speak,
She found within this northern land what many dare not seek.

**TRIBUTE TO THE HERB TOWN TRAILBLAZERS**

"Blackie" Brooks, Charlie Krug, the Kobars and the Kerrs,
Prospectors and pioneers and trappers of the furs.

Charlie Vance, the Vickers clan, Charles Stayback and Dion,
These were men who had the strength to push and carry on.

LaChapelle and Bordeaux, McDonald and Durand,
Manitoba Northerners, settlers of our land.

Paterson and Ferguson, Kate Rice and "Billie" Wedge,
All voyageurs and wanderers, thrived on danger's edge.

Angus Woods, Billy Todd, Sam Kluklatch, Jack Mosso,
The Bartletts and the Stoltzes, all paved this path we know.

The Bryentons, Bill English, Dick Ellice and George Doll,
Pioneers unknown to me; we owe them one and all.

## GEAR JAMMIN'

The highway stretches far beyond the dreams of any man,
I'll chase the ends of foreign roads to freedom if I can.
The passion of the power-stroke that throbs between my legs
Responds to twist of throttle grip, feet firmly on the pegs.

The leather breaks the surface of a wind that warms my soul,
Hobnailed boots give comfort in the quest toward my goal.
The freedom of the open road, hot blood within my veins,
Wheels rotate with shiny spin, spurred on by greasy chains.

Rubber grips the asphalt with a bond that I can trust,
The engine throbs with freedom, power in its thrust.
The thunder of this iron horse is music to my ears,
I roll on down the open road, jammin' through the gears.

## HOMELESS

I'm old and I'm tired and near sick to death
Of the city's foul stench and my own rancid breath.
The rush of the traffic polluting the earth,
The grey concrete jungle, empty of mirth,
The soul-twisting pain of lifelong regrets,
And my family garden, dead from neglect.

If ever a man deserved a worse fate,
I'd look in his eyes and offer him hate.
For hate's close to pity and pity I've none,
Spent in the balance of battles not won.
Never again I vowed long ago,
Would I show any weakness to friend or to foe.

Crippled in spirit, infirm with age,
I stifle yet fuel the impotent rage
That gnaws at my guts, eats at my brain,
Devours my conscience again and again.
The yellow smog sullies the oncoming dawn
As this cold, cursed life goes on and goes on.

I am a man who has gambled and lost,
Who has followed false lovers, not counting the cost.
I've fed all my vices, indulged in taboos,
My future I've traded for a bottle of booze.
Gave up my wife, my son and his hugs,
Cashed in my soul for a handful of drugs.

So weary am I and bereft of the will
To carry the torch and struggle on still,
I've lost all my lust and love for this life,
The loneliness cuts like a fresh-sharpened knife
That stabs to the core and slices the breast;
I pray for the moment my soul comes to rest.

## THE HEADFRAME

The headframe guards the landscape like a sentinel of steel,
Promising prosperity to those who know the feel
Of muckers' boots and slicker suits, the hammer of jackleg steel.

The headlamps cast an eerie glow beneath this earthy crust,
Stabbing light illuminates, revealing smoke and dust,
As miners trudge through muck and sludge to labour as they must.

The ore vein lies in stringers, encased in waste of old,
Beneath the hard rock surface, obscured in seamy folds
Of biotite and magnetite, the guardians of the gold.

## FLIN FLON ON THE ROCK

Flin Flon on its rounded rock, its ancient sulphide base,
Stands strong and tall with hardy flock, steel sentinel in place.
Headframe guards the collar house on Creighton's eastern side,
Copper mined from deep decline produced with miner's pride.

Smokestack spears the northern sky, spews out sulphur waste,
Yellow cloud of sullen smear deposits bitter taste.
Honest folk of hardy seed, they stem from pioneer stock,
Copper earth, my place of birth, Flin Flon on the rock.

## LOVE AT FIRST FIGHT

The trapper was a knapper of the finest furs in town,
Eagle feathered cap of leather graced his balding crown.
With lotion and a potion and a notion for his art,
This skinner was a winner, and his name was Jacques Lafarte.

The diner for the miners served the best grub in the land,
Jacques hungered for the company and coffee on demand,
Had a passion for the fashion of a hearty home-cooked meal;
He never dreamed his lust for food could hold such sex appeal.

A woman as a miner might to some seem quite obscene,
But a stoper and a jackleg were the tools of Miss Maxine.
This diner for the miners was the finest spot around,
In mini-skirt and flannel shirt, she ate her roast beef ground.

Jacques studied her and muddied up his coffee with some cream,
Gazed at Max the miner, was immersed in lover's dream.
She stared right back at his attack upon her maiden charms,
Threw a glass, yelled, "Kiss my ass!" and punched him in the arm.

The trapper was a scrapper, and he loved to throw his fists,
He seldom lost a bar room brawl, his right hook never missed.
He ranted and he panted and he planted both his feet,
He cussed her and he flustered in the face of sure defeat.

The trapper had the miner fixed beneath his grimy glare,
The miner with eyeliner just returned his steely stare.
They muscled and they wrestled, then they tussled in the dirt,
The trapper caught a slapper in the ear - it really hurt.

The miner had a shiner and a cut across her nose,
Threw off her bloody flannel shirt, surveyed her pantyhose,
A musser and a fusser and a girl of strange design,
She stammered as she hammered at the man not from the mine.

Now, the preacher was a screecher, and he laid down heavy laws,
Saw the scene and intervened with reason for just cause,
Gave a slap to trapper's back, grabbed the miner's head,
"There is no course but true remorse," the holy preacher said.

The preacher was a teacher, so he urged the two to wed,
Kicked the trapper on his crapper and released the miner's head,
Then he slowly took his holy book and opened it with awe,
The teacher now turned preacher screeched out holy law.

The trapper and the miner held their hands up in the air,
A tremble and a quiver in their voices of despair,
They pleaded and they wheedled and created quite a scene,
The scrapper of a trapper and the miner named Maxine.

The miner was no whiner and no finer fight was seen,
The trapper rubbed his crapper where the preacher's boot had been,
Took miner's hand in rough demand and begged her to be his,
Kissed Maxine in steamy scene, lived on in wedded bliss.

## SHORES OF WEKUSKO

Along the shores of Wekusko, just north of old Herb Town,
A graveyard lies in brambles, and beneath its thorny crown,
Rest the ghosts of pioneers, sleeping in the ground.

A little farther up the shore, you'll see Laguna's waste,
It lies in level low-grade, and projects a rocky base,
A monument to lives it took, etched on forest's face.

I paddle now 'cross Crow Duck Bay to land on sandy loam,
I sense the spirit of voyageurs never more to roam;
I cherish this wild beauty; I'm proud to call it home.

## WAITING

In a far northern land, there still lives a man
Who keeps his dreams held close at hand.
He remembers his lover, so gentle and kind,
A vision of beauty he long hoped to find.
As fair as the wind that midsummer brings,
As tender and soft as the first buds of spring.
As golden and brief as the colours of fall,
Their time spent together was not long at all.

Now winter's at hand in this white, frozen land,
And the Northern Lights dance in a wide, milky band.
He thinks of this woman who so touched his life,
And he feels such a need to make her his wife.
But with little to offer, his hope slips away,
Though his love for her grows with each passing day.
In a far northern land, there still waits a man,
His mind is quite open, his heart in his hands.

## BALLAD OF MISS RIGGS

He came in from the cold, and this story he told,
Of romance, riches and greed.
He was brassy and bold, had a pouch full of gold,
On the bar laid his prospector's deed.
He shook snow from his boots, with a gallant salute,
Bought a round of beers for the boys.
He paid from his poke, and I tell you no joke,
The sight of it hushed all the noise.

"This paper gives right to those who have might,
To search the shores of Great Bear
For the black golden grains that litter the plains,
And the lode that's sure to be there.
So I staked out my claim with visions of fame,
For I'd found a fair nugget or two.
I built a small shack with the sweat off my back,
And panned with a vigour that grew.

The winter's first snow was starting to blow
'Cross the tundra, that treeless domain,
And I needed enough of that bright yellow stuff
To hold me till spring came again.
So with fast fading light, I toiled through the night,
Until finally ice froze my digs,
Then I packed up my gear and headed straight here,
To ask for the hand of Miss Riggs."

"Ramone's gone away to the dance hall," I say,
"In Dawson, at Big Jim's behest.
He offered her pearls to be one of the girls,
To please any man's rude requests."
The man lost his grin as the knowledge seeped in,
He sagged at the shoulders and wept.
Laid his head on the bar, with voice from afar
Asked, "How long has this secret been kept?"

"The very next day after you went away,
Big Jim and Ramone hit the trail.
She left you this note, and from it I quote,
'Good-bye, for I know you will fail.'"
The tears in his eyes he could not disguise,
He sobbed as if stabbed to the core.
He rolled up his claim and put it to flame,
And scattered his gold on the floor.

"It's not of much use," cried the now mad recluse,
As his eyes quickly searched for the door.
Not a man met his stare as he laid his soul bare,
For his hand held a Colt forty-four.
He crossed the hushed room filled with the gloom
Of a man that's more dead than not,
He strode out the door with his forty-four bore.
The next thing we heard was a shot.

We buried him there, by the shore of Great Bear,
With a marker of high granite stones.
For wolves have their say at the end of the day,
And would rip the flesh from his bones.
He never gained fame, nor gave us his name,
That man who came in from the cold;
So we raised up a toast to his premature ghost,
And divided his nuggets of gold.

## THE HUNT

The night sky is lit with a wide, milky band,
The moon round and full, the hour is at hand
When shadowy beasts come stalking in packs,
Sniffing at spoor, searching for tracks.

Howling with hungering, haunting lament,
The timber wolves gather with deathly intent.
The grey one barks orders, short-tempered and vexed;
They must kill tonight to survive till the next.

They pick up the scent of a cow and her calf,
The leader then splits the party in half.
Rolof and One-Eye, Sheba and Queen,
Flank to the left where the tracks were last seen.

Grey-One with cunning, Brutus with might,
Burst through the snow drifts, running full flight.
They lessen the distance 'tween hunter and prey
As the rest of the pack fall into the fray.

The moose lashes out in its panic and fear
As Sheba attacks the cow from the rear.
One-Eye, more wary, goes for the calf;
The mother's sharp hooves near rip him in half.

Brutus moves in and snaps his jaws closed
With deadly precision around the cow's nose.
Grey-One tears deep at the base of the throat,
The hot blood of life spills over his coat.

Rolof and Queen catch up to the calf,
The kill is soon over, for such is their craft.
Much learned of life and practised in death,
They howl in success with blood-frosted breath.

The cubs will not hunger this cold winter's night,
The grey pack of hunters has conquered its plight.
Now as the full moon lights up the sky,
They sing their refrain, a haunting reply.

## DEATH BY DRUNKEN DRIVER

It's not enough that you're forced to suffer
At the hands of a blind, reckless stranger,
The destruction and loss, the grief and the cost
Of this drunkard's indifference to danger.
The drunkard escaped with his life, and he'll take
Whatever this life has to offer,
Regret and remorse are par for the course,
But cannot fill life's empty coffer.

It's not enough that you're forced to suffer
When reality slowly seeps through
That grim, misty fog, the heart-wrenching sob
When you know through your tears that it's true.
It's not enough that you're forced to suffer
When death drains your life like a sieve,
It's not enough, no not near enough:
For now you must go on and live.

## LITTLE TIN BOX

The drifter blew in, sat down with chagrin,
Scattered some coins on the bar,
The spittle ran thin to the edge of his chin,
He chewed on a stubby cigar.

His stetson was rumpled, overcoat crumpled,
The hair bristled out of his nose,
He dug in his ear, ordered a beer,
Then looked 'round to see how it goes.

With hearty good cheer, a glass full of beer,
The bartender served to his guest,
Who drank half of it down, grimaced and frowned,
Then scratched at some deep-seated pest.

With belch and a burp, a slather and slurp,
The drifter chugged down the cold beer,
He chewed his cigar till the end was like tar,
Then swallowed the stub with a sneer.

He reached in his coat, the grizzled old goat
(I swear you could smell the man's socks),
With reverent care and a steely eyed stare,
He brought out a little tin box.

"All that I own or profess to have known,
Is contained in this small metal tin,
I harbour it well, my safeguard from hell,"
The drifter confessed with a grin.

"I'll trade it to you for another cold brew,
My sorry excuse for a friend,
It's a hot, dusty day, I've walked a long way,
Now my journey has come to an end."

The barkeep surveyed the eyes dull and greyed,
And saw to the depths of the soul,
He practised his craft and poured out cold draft,
Dispensed with a flourish and roll.

"I've looked in your eyes, and it's fair to surmise
You're a man with a penchant for drink;
I'll take up your deal, here's five for a meal,"
The bartender said with a wink.

"I thank you so much for your kindness and such."
The drifter said not a word more,
He swallowed his brew, gazed down at his shoe,
Dropped dead on the dirty bar floor.

The patrons were loud, a bold, raucous crowd,
But at this point they suddenly fled,
A doctor was called, robust and ribald;
He pronounced the drifter quite dead.

After the death, the drifter's last breath,
The bartender opened the box;
A photo within, a cameo pin,
A little girl's blonde curly locks.

## LOVE

Love is the essence of trust and respect
Over the years with no fear of neglect,
Fire the flame with faith and desire,
In such a short time we'll climb even higher.

With hopes for our future as bright as the sun,
And dreams of the day when we will be one,
Instill in my heart a love that is pure,
Never to fail, for we will endure.

## RED

She had flaming red hair and a definite flair,
Her smile could make Northern Lights dance,
Her eyes of pale blue, a wondrous hue,
Invited a man to romance.
She was thoughtful and kind, with love that was blind,
Convinced of a good life to come.
Married early in life, she made a good wife,
But the bastard she wed was a bum.

He drank like a fish and all of us wish
He would not have played poker that night.
He'd constantly lose on account of the booze,
And often that prompted a fight.
He started to swear at the cards that lay there,
But the curse got stuck in his craw.
He turned to the right as she came into sight,
And witnessed what everyone saw.

She had flaming red hair and an icy cold stare
As she boldly stepped into the room.
She glared at the man with cards in his hand,
Her eyes flashed hellfire and doom.
"I've been a good wife, and hoped for a life
Free of your drunken deceit.
Well, I've had enough," she said in a huff,
"Your bags are out in the street."

He withered and shrank while the rest of us drank,
For there wasn't much more we could do.
She cursed him again and made it quite plain
She was starting to live life anew.
She stuck out her hand, took off the gold band,
And threw it right into his face.
"Never no more will you darken my door,
May hell be a comforting place!"

She had flaming red hair and a definite flair
As she gracefully strode to the street.
Her eyes held the pride of love truly tried,
Unwilling to suffer defeat.
She changed her life's course, no fear or remorse,
For happier days lay ahead . . .
She knows there's a chance of lovers' romance,
If only she picks me instead.

## SOLITARY CHRISTMAS

On a cold Christmas Eve, in a cabin on a hill,
The trapper prepared to skin his last kill.
He brought out his whetstone and spit on it twice,
Selected a knife and scratched at his lice,
Then swore at the dog, asleep on the rug,
"You flea-bitten hound, you've given me bugs!"
He sat down and stroked cold steel against stone
Till the blade was so sharp it would slice to the bone.

He stepped to the table where the body lay cold,
The poor beast was stiffening as rigour took hold.
It was hairy and fat and had horns like a deer,
But the hooves had small wings, and wasn't it queer
How the eyes gleamed with light, and look at that nose,
So big and so bulbous, so red that it glows!
"A strange looking creature, not seen one before,
It will bring me great fame, and riches galore."

With eyes full of glee and a murderous grin,
The mad trapper expertly stuck the knife in.
As the blood from the carcass seeped to the floor,
A terrible pounding came from the door.
The dog growled in fear and hid out of sight,
For who would come calling this cold winter's night?
The trapper, he bellowed and lunged with a roar,
The knife in his hands all covered in gore.

But before he could reach it, the door crashed to bits,
And the madman recoiled as he lost all his wits.
He started to gag and retch and get sick,
For he knew this intruder, they called him Saint Nick!
The trapper awoke, in a sweat, with a scream,
Not knowing at first it was only a dream.
Staring in darkness, he pondered this thought:
In solitary madness, such dreams are wrought.

## CHAINED WARRIOR

The grizzled old biker hunched down on one knee,
The bones in his hands like a gnarled, twisted tree.
He sneered as the spittle dripped down from his lips,
Pulled the shank from his guts, on his own blood he slipped.

Regaining his balance as three bandits stared,
They thought he was dead, but he stood and he glared
At the trio of punks and their murderous sin.
They ganged round the warrior to do the man in.

The old man lashed out with his contraband knife,
The closest one dropped and spilled out his life
From a wound in his throat, so ragged and raw.
He died as he choked on the blood in his craw.

The second, a street fighter, feet set apart,
Jerked and convulsed from a blow to the heart.
The last one, alone in this "family" of three,
Gave up the battle and screamed out a plea.

The warrior, he heard not, he cared not, he killed,
He struck the punk's eye and the cavity filled
With six inches of steel, to the hilt of the shank.
The last bandit's future went totally blank.

The grizzled old biker staggered and fell
To his bunk in the corner of the dank, dirty cell.
In his pain and his fury, he dreamed for a while,
Of his bike, then his woman, and died with a smile.

BS

## About the Illustrator

*Robert M. Southern was born in 1958 in Campbellford, Ontario and raised in Bancroft, Ontario. He moved to Snow Lake in 1979 and is currently employed in the mining industry. Mr. Southern, who began drawing in grade school, has exhibited his work at Northern Juried Art Shows. His mural honouring Samuel Hearne can be seen in Snow Lake. His artwork is testimony to his love of nature and the North.*

Additional copies of ***RHYMES & BALLADS FROM BERRY BAY*** are available at a cost of $15.00 per book (includes postage and handling). Allow 4 to 6 weeks for delivery. Please make cheques or money orders payable to R. Crone. Send orders to:

***RHYMES & BALLADS FROM BERRY BAY***

P.O. Box 867

Snow Lake, Manitoba R0B 1M0

Canada

* * * * *